FI[illegible]NER

WHAT YOU NEED TO KNOW BEFORE YOU BUY YOUR FIRST HORSE

By

Carolynn Marshall

FIRST-TIME HORSE OWNER

WHAT YOU NEED TO KNOW
BEFORE YOU BUY YOUR FIRST HORSE

TABLE OF CONTENTS

I.

FIRST-TIME HORSE OWNER

WHAT YOU NEED TO KNOW BEFORE YOU BUY YOUR FIRST HORSE

INTRODUCTION

Buying a horse will be one of the most important decisions you make in your life. "Really?" you ask. Really. This may be more important than deciding what car to buy or more important than deciding on what house or apartment to live in. Maybe not as important as deciding to have a child, but almost!

Bringing any animal into your life is a pretty big commitment. That animal will depend on you for its well-being and quality of life. Providing a horse with what it needs for good health, safety, and good living conditions is no easy task. And this dependent relationship with your horse will probably last many years, 10, 15 even 20 or more. Most horse owners deeply love their animals and will tell you the commitment is worth every bit of time, energy and money that they spend.

Sad to say, too many horse owners buy a horse for the wrong reasons or with too little information. For these people, having a horse will likely be an unhappy and expensive experience for both the owner and the animal.

This book covers important basics that will help the first-time horse owner make decisions about riding and about buying a horse. At the end of each chapter, space is provided for you to jot notes about the chapter highlights. This will reinforce the information and give you an easy reference for review later. Points made in each chapter are illustrated by one or more true stories. These stories are both entertaining and instructive.

Please note that I am not a horse trainer, famous or otherwise. But, I have had 20 plus years of experience with horses. This book is intended to help a beginner get started and to provide you with a "heads up" about horses. It is written with the highest hopes that you will be a happy horse owner who says with joy, "I have a horse!"

II.

MAKING THE DECISION TO OWN A HORSE

You want to ride of course! Right? Right! You might also be thinking, horses are magnificent creatures and it would be a thrill to own one. That's a really good reason too. Maybe you were in love with horses from a young age but didn't have the opportunity to ride or own one. For the first-time horse owner, your answer to the question, "Why do you want a horse?" is going to determine your eventual happiness and satisfaction with having one.

You might be thinking of a horse as another pet. If so you are in for some big (as in horse size) surprises. A horse is not like a dog, a cat, a bird, or other common household pet. A horse's needs and psychology are very different from the usual pet.

Although horses have been domesticated, they retain their natural instincts for survival in the wild. In some horses this is stronger than in others. Still, it is important to never forget the saying, "A horse is a horse." When startled or fearful, it is a powerful animal. Be sure to learn how to handle horses before you buy one! In the following chapters you will read more about this and how to go about it.

If you take for granted that a horse is to ride, end of story, your horse experience might not go well at all. While most activities with horses do involve riding it, different breeds were developed over the centuries to perform varying tasks. Within the breed, different lines can be specialized. For instance, there are Quarter Horses that race, that work cattle, that are sport horses involving speed and agility such as barrel racing. Often this breed makes a very nice trail riding horse.

So what kinds of jobs do horses have and which of those jobs suits your temperament, time, and monetary resources? Here is a partial list to consider as you think about why you want a horse.

- Trail riding
- Arena work
- Parades
- Cow work
- Barrel racing
- Dressage
- Jumping
- Reining
- Endurance riding
- Cross country or fox hunting
- Polo

Each of these tasks requires a horse with a specific temperament, physicality, health and training. For instance, not all horses are suited for dressage or jumping and English style is very different from Western style. Some horses hate arena work; others are so "hot" it takes a long time, at greater risk, to use them for trail riding. There are horses that are very versatile and do more than one job well, but some horses don't and will be better suited for one discipline.

So the question, "Why do you want a horse?" really means "What is your plan for this new addition to your life?" As mentioned, part of your plan is to determine what kind of riding you will enjoy over the years of owning your horse. It may be that you'd like to go on trail rides, and you'd also like to do horse shows that require arena work. Or, you may know in your heart you'd love to compete in endurance riding which takes place over many miles and hours in the saddle.

If you're not sure what discipline you will be happiest doing, before you buy your horse take time to research a variety of the jobs that horses do. There are many articles and books on these subjects, and horse shows are common events. Look for shows in your area that feature dressage, jumping, English and Western classes. (Many tack and feed stores carry "The Horse Trader," an equine newspaper. It is free and lists activities being held in your area.) Usually entrance to watch is free, and this is a good way to find the activity that captures your heart. This is a good way to locate trainers as well, since most of the participants will be there with their trainers. Most trainers are happy to talk to interested visitors who may end up being a client.

Whatever you decide about what you want to do with your horse, rest assured that it is absolutely okay. Don't be persuaded into doing what someone else thinks you should want to do. For example, it really is okay if you only want to ride your horse in an arena and have no interest at all in trail riding. Good for you! There's a horse out there that will be very happy to work with you in the arena. A horse will be your willing partner if you give it a job that you both enjoy doing.

Too many would be horse owners rush into their decision and buy a horse based on wrong factors, such as how pretty it is. Buying a horse this way is guaranteed to bring problems. It is really worth taking your time and doing it right. Reading this book will be a good start and it will give you a much better chance of finding your ideal horse.

* * * * * * * * * * * * * * *

My Story:

I think I was born with a “loves horses” gene. From the first pony ride, I wanted my own horse. My family couldn’t afford that, but I was lucky to have friends and family members with horses. In those days, as a youngster, I just got on and rode the horse. Sometimes bareback, if in a saddle a borrowed one, I rode with other kids. We didn’t take lessons, we didn’t read books about it. We rode with total trust and joy. We rode in dry river beds and even in parades. The adults took for granted that we would be safe, and somehow none of the kids I rode with ever got hurt.

I think there was a good deal of luck involved. One of my rides bolted towards an orange grove, but luckily stopped before we got to the trees. Another time I thought it would be fun to try “Roman riding” where you stand on the horse’s back. I got promptly bucked off!

As a middle-aged adult and empty-nester, I decided to get back to my first love, horses. I was so fortunate to be introduced to “Shadow.” She was a 16-year-old Appaloosa and as pretty as they come. But more importantly, she had a “cool” temperament and a willing nature. I rode with friends and with Shadow’s owner who knew she was the right horse for someone like me.

For the four years I rode Shadow I didn't have any accidents. Good yes, but I proceeded to buy my own horse with a false sense of confidence and without knowing how to find another Shadow. I still had not taken any lessons but I did take a lot for granted!

My American Paint Horse, Doll, was a jittery mare with little training. With persistence and a number of trainers, we did local shows and even won two high-point buckles. But we couldn't advance to higher-level shows because Western Pleasure was not a good job for Doll. She wasn't slow enough or calm enough.

I learned after owning Doll several years that she loved working cows. She was bred for it. Unfortunately, it was too late to become committed to competing in that sport. Doll was getting older and I was already invested in other training.

I found out the hard way that Doll was not the best horse for trail riding. She was always alert and easily startled. If something scary surprised her, she would spin in preparation to flee. Many times I came out of the saddle, and once I ended up with a broken collarbone. Another time I broke an ankle.

I kept Doll in spite the challenges she presented. After 15 years, we've found a groove. I became a good rider, but I should have found a safer way to go about it!

NOTES

III.

BEFORE YOU BUY YOUR HORSE

If you are an inexperienced beginner rider, your first and most important preparation is to take riding lessons. Plan on taking lessons for at least a year, or even better take lessons for two years, before you buy your own horse. If you have made the decision to get a horse it may be difficult to delay your desire for one. By putting it off for a while, you ultimately will be much happier with the end result.

Taking lessons will expose you to different breeds of horses and also the differences in gender. Generally speaking, geldings are more predictable than mares. Stallions are rarely used as pleasure horses and should be used by experienced horse handlers. Various breeds are suited to the various disciplines. A good trainer can help you sort out what breed is going to be best for the type of riding you want to do.

After taking sufficient lessons, and if your trainer agrees, a next step worth considering is a lease agreement for a horse. Most stables have people interested in leasing, or doing a half-lease, with their horse. Also, consider a lease with an option to buy. With a lease you won't have the up-front cost of buying a horse, and usually the owner will pay for any vet bills and shoeing. By leasing, you will find out the demands on your time and energy that caring for a horse makes. With at least a one-month lease prior to buying, you will learn a lot about the horse. When you make the purchase you can be more confident it is the right horse for you.

It's a good idea to have a stables lined up at the time of your purchase. If you primarily want to do trail riding check the stables in your area and ask if there is easy access to trails. At some point you may decide to buy a truck and horse trailer so you can take your horse to a variety of trails, but for starters you will want trails to ride on by the stables. Not all stables have access to trails!

If you want to specialize and compete in a particular discipline, such as dressage or jumping, find a stables that has trainers for that discipline. Spend time talking to those trainers and tell them what you have in mind. A good trainer can help you find a horse that suits your level of experience and your budget.

Another part of good preparation is to read as much as you can. There is a lifetime of learning when it comes to horses. Be sure to learn the main body parts of a horse, as this will be helpful when talking to your trainer and your vet about any issues, concerns or questions you may have.

Another important consideration is finding a horse that you won't out-grow. Too many times a novice rider finds the right, safer horse for the early stages of becoming an equestrian, but becomes bored when the horse isn't capable of doing more. It will be more satisfying in the long run if you spend enough time on various lesson horses and leased horses to become an intermediate rider. Then you will be ready to pick a horse that can be a fun and interesting partner for years to come.

If you do buy an older horse that you feel is safer for your current ability, it can be a really good starter horse.

However, try to prepare yourself for giving that horse up. Within several years it is likely you may feel frustrated because the horse world is opening up for you but your horse isn't capable of doing more. Or, the horse is now aged and starts to have health issues that are incapacitating, expensive and possibly career ending. You may find that the horse has to be retired.

* * * * * * * * * * * * * * *

My Story:

I found Doll at a local stable. I knew I wanted a Paint or an Appaloosa. I knew I wanted to start showing and my only experience was in Western riding.

The person selling Doll presented herself as a trainer who worked with people showing Western. It turned out she worked with the teens at the stables who had well-trained horses. I learned later that the trainer was selling Doll because she wasn't trained or particularly suited for those riders or for Western showing. I was in too big a hurry to spend time learning more about the trainer or the horse.

One Western show trainer wanted me to sell Doll and get a horse more suited to high-level showing. I decided to keep my horse and moved to another stables and trainer.

I was convinced that with enough work, effort, and practice we could succeed. We did win our share of ribbons in lower-level shows. However we were not competitive against horses bred with the cool, somewhat lazy temperament of the western pleasure show horse. Doll would have been happier with English riding or work with cows The lesson here is to take the time to know what you enjoy most and find out what type of horse or breed to purchase.

NOTES

IV.

WHAT WILL YOUR HORSE NEED?

This chapter provides a quick summary of what your horse needs in order to stay healthy and rideable. If you have leased a horse you may have some understanding of this subject. If you have taken lessons but not had the full responsibility of horse care, this will give you a good overview.

Shelter and feed would be at the top of the list for horse care. Surprisingly, horses can do well in an open pasture as well as the confined space of a box stall. But, both of those options have contingencies.

A pastured horse may not be the best riding horse. If it is with other horses, it may take on the herd psychology. Issues of dominance will be in play. If your horse is dominant in the herd, it will be dominant with you. If it is lower on the pecking order, it may get kicked and bitten a lot which could lead to more vet bills. It may be difficult to catch when you want to ride. It most likely will be dirty most of the time since horses love to roll in the dirt.

A horse in a box stall will need arrangements for getting out daily. Most stables have a round pen which is used for exercising and training horses. If you ride daily for an hour, or work your horse in the round pen, that may be enough for a horse stabled in a box stall. Some horses love their little homes and are quite comfortable. Others are easily bored in the small space with little contact with other horses. These horses develop bad habits, including "weaving" (rocking to and fro) and "cribbing" (biting the stall door). For them, more exercise might help, or a cribbing collar (a device that discourages that behavior).

The ideal shelter for most horses is called an "in and out." This provides an area that is covered, where both the horse and its feed will stay dry, and an area that is open air so the horse gets plenty of sunshine and can visit with its neighbors.

Regarding feed, when you purchase your horse find out what it is currently being fed. Initially you will want to continue the same diet, and you will need to check with your stables to see what feed is available.

At different stages of its life, and depending on the job your horse is doing, its diet will most likely change over time. There are many varieties of hay. Hay is also sold in a pelleted form, which is easier to chew and to digest. Hay quality is not easy to determine. Many owners give their horses supplements to ensure their animals have their nutritional needs met. It is a good practice to discuss your horse's diet with a trainer if you are working with one, and with your veterinarian.

Taking care of your horse's hooves is a must. It may sound tired and trite, but the saying "no hoof, no horse" is so true. If the horse's hooves fail to function properly, the horse will be in so much pain it cannot be ridden and often it has to be put down.

It will be extremely helpful over the lifetime of your horse if you can find and develop a relationship with a skillful, reliable farrier or shoer. Many horse owners opt for the cheapest one in an effort to reduce the cost of owning a horse. This is probably the worst cost to trim. Ask trainers, the stable owner, and other people boarding their horses at your stables who they think is the best farrier.

Some farriers specialize in the needs of various breeds, such as Tennessee Walkers or racehorses. Some specialize in keeping the hoof as natural as possible and only trim but do not put on shoes. Also, some horses have special needs such as pads under their shoes. Again, trainers and vets can help you determine the particular shoeing needs of your horse.

While grooming may not technically be a "need" of horses (for instance, wild horses are never groomed), the time spent grooming your horse is time well spent. During grooming you will notice if there are any changes in the horse's feet or coat. You will find if there are any cuts or indications of health problems, such as weight loss. Also, you will note if there seems to be soreness or discomfort as you brush over the coat. Horses are usually sprayed with a hose if they are sweaty after riding if the weather permits. A bath with soap and water is only needed occasionally to thoroughly clean your horse. Show horses may be bathed more frequently and have specialized grooming.

Lastly, on the basic needs of your horse, is the topic of vaccinations and parasite control. Many stables require a regimen for all boarded horses that includes certain vaccinations and regular worming. This requirement makes sense when many animals are in such close proximity. Without vaccinations, if one horse develops a contagious disease it can spread easily. Parasites are common in horses and if they are not controlled the animal will become thin and listless. It is helpful to keep a record of your horse's health. See the first year health record provided.

It is very helpful to have a selection of books in your home library that deal with horse ailments. Look over the table of contents and read up on common problems. That way, you can become sensitive to the signs of a problem. For instance, a horse that is starting to colic may not want to get up. It may have stopped eating and may hang it's head and look ill. The horse usually stops producing manure because there is a blockage of some kind. If it is in pain, the horse may lift a hind leg and kick towards its side or it may lay down and roll from side to side. A horse that has the flu will keep eating and making manure. It will have a fever and will not look well or act "normal."

It is also helpful to subscribe to magazines from the horse world. These can be online subscriptions or home delivered paper ones. The more you can read and learn about horse training and care, the better prepared you will be to take good care of your equine partner.

* * * * * * * * * * * * * * *

My Story:

Over the years I have moved Doll to various stables and trainers. At one facility, she never settled. She paced and pawed holes in her stall. She didn't like the feed that was given. After a month I had to move her since it just wasn't working out.

As soon as I took her to the new place and she walked into her box stall, Doll sighed happily and calmed down immediately. Horses can be that sensitive to their surroundings. Sometimes a horse will stop eating and drinking water because it is depressed in the situation. I have seen horses that get so bonded to a partner horse that they can't be separated. If at the same stables they will call and call to each other if they are not stabled in stalls next to each other. If one horse is taken out for a ride the other begins calling for it.

From my experience I would describe farriers as mostly a highly independent group. It can be difficult to find one that is talented at this trade and reliable. Horses usually need their feet done every 6 to 8 weeks, and I have had more than one farrier disappear and not show up for 10 weeks. Doll once had a hoof emergency and I needed the farrier to come as soon as possible to pull her shoes off. The farrier never returned my urgent calls. I had to have a foreman at the stables pull her shoes. Luckily he was able to do it but it was not his job or his training to do so.

NOTES

V.

BASICS ABOUT EQUIPMENT

If you spend time around a stables, you may be introduced to various grooming tools such as brushes and hoof picks. Other than that, you probably won't have much experience with bridles, bits or saddles. Usually when taking lessons the horse is saddled and ready to go, so that all you do is get on it and take the lesson. If you are lucky, you'll be allowed to groom your mount at some point. Ask for this privilege and ask to be taught how to saddle a horse. I can't count how many people I've met that get a horse but don't know how to put the saddle and bridle on!

When you buy a horse, the owners may have a saddle, blanket and bridle they are willing to sell you. This may be okay for starters, but more often you will end up buying your own equipment.

A saddle has to fit both you and the horse. There are saddles specialized for various types of riding: English, Western, Roping, Reining, Barrel Racing, etc. A trainer or your local tack and feed store can help you choose and fit a saddle for you and your horse. Circle Y is a trusted Western brand and saddle maker. Whatever the brand, plan to sit in a number of saddles until you find the right one for you.

Next you will need to determine the shape that is good for your horse. Be aware that different breeds are built differently. For instance, some saddles are specially designed for Arabians and Tennessee Walkers. The wrong saddle fit can cause saddle sores which are painful for the horse and will result in less riding time for you. Depending on your budget, you may be able to find a good used saddle that fits both you and the horse well enough to be your beginning saddle. A good new saddle can easily cost $1500 or much more.

Saddle blankets are necessary to cushion the saddle on the horse's back and to keep the saddle from rubbing off the horse's hair. An ill fitting saddle and/or blanket can make "saddle sores" and if that happens you can't ride until the sores heal. Picking out these items and fitting them properly is very important. There are a variety of cinches to choose from, so again talk to others about the choices they made. Some people like a cinch covered with sheepskin. I have used a neoprene cinch for many years. However, these don't work for all horses. The wrong cinch can also cause sores.

Bridles and bits require as much attention as saddles and blankets. Bridles can have one ear, two ears or a headband. They come in different sizes, including pony size, Arab size, regular horse size, and large. The bit attaches to the bridle and it has to fit properly in the horse's mouth to work effectively. Not all horses' mouths are identical. Some have higher roofs to their mouth and their teeth can affect the fit of the bit. I tried many bits before I found the one that my horse was most comfortable in.

Reins are separate from the bridle and attach to it. It may be surprising to learn that there are many types of reins. Both ends of a "single rein" attach to the bridle, so it is continuous with no break or separation. There are reins made of rope and of leather. Some are thick, and some are thin. I prefer heavier weight, leather reins. I found when I tried the rope reins I developed the symptoms of carpel tunnel, and my wrists would be sore. Also I like "split reins," which are two separate reins that each attach to the bit. I find that split reins are more versatile.

There is great information out there about bits and how to choose the correct one for your horse. I prefer Myler and you can go online to find out about their design. Some tack stores will let you try several as long as the ones you return are not scratched or damaged in the process. Or, you may want to try used bits before buying a new one so you won't spend so much money trying to find the best one.

There are many other pieces of equipment to consider besides saddles, saddle blankets, bridles and bits. A winter blanket makes sense sometimes, depending on how cold it gets at night and if your horse has much of a winter coat. Horses burn fat to stay warm in cold weather, so you may be able to skip a blanket but find you need to feed your horse more calories in the winter.

Day sheets are light weight blankets that are used primarily to keep a horse clean when it is turned out of its stall. Tail wraps protect the horse's tail. Various "boots" protect the horse's legs and around the hooves. I have used all of this stuff at one time or another, but gradually decided I didn't really need any of it. Wait before buying these items to determine if your horse will really benefit. It all costs money, and can add up quickly if you are not selective.

One item I really like having in my tack room is my horse's "cooler." You will have to learn when and how to use this item. I like it for when my horse is sweaty or I have hosed her off and it is a very cool day. With a cooler on, she will dry quickly.

Be sure to have a medicine kit with your tack. It should include a thermometer, vet wrap, antibiotic ointment, wound cleanser, thrush medication, Vaseline, any medications that your horse takes routinely, "bute" (or other type of horse aspirin), and Banamine. You can get bute and Banamine from your vet who will explain when they are useful.

Leg wraps have many different purposes and there are different types of them. It is important to learn how to properly apply wraps. If applied incorrectly, you can make your horse go lame and the recovery period can be many months.

Last but not least, you will need halters and lead lines. Look into the various styles and uses. There are heavy duty halters, rope halters, leather halters, and show halters. I have one of each. This is a piece of equipment you will most likely use every day. They come in various sizes. Choose a halter that will fit your horse and a lead line that is comfortable for you to hold. Consider buying gloves and using them when you are handling your horse.

* * * * * * * * * * * * * * *

My Story:

I purchased a western show saddle and another western saddle that I planned to use for trail riding. Both were quality saddles that fit my horse and were comfortable for me. Over several years, on trail rides, Doll would spook at something and spin away from it. More than once, I would come out of my trail saddle and land on the ground. When we retired from showing, I found that I liked my show saddle best. I started using it for trail rides and discovered that when Doll spooked, I was able to stay in that saddle. I ended up selling the trail saddle and have used the show saddle for 15 years. Lesson learned: It's possible that one saddle is all you need. Talk to other horse owners and find out why they chose the saddle they are using.

NOTES

VI.

WHEN IT'S TIME TO BUY YOUR HORSE

After all of the considerations in the previous chapters have been thought about, checked out, accomplished and arranged you're ready to start looking for your horse! In this process you probably have a pretty good idea of the price range you are comfortable with. Now it's time to see what's available.

Here are things to think about for starting your search:

If you want a horse that will be your riding partner for many years, the age of the animal will be important. A young horse, say a 5 - or 6 – year old, could be a 20-year member of your family.

A young horse is likely to have less training and could require a very skillful rider. So it is important to be realistic about your riding abilities. It is possible to find a younger horse with an absolutely calm, accepting temperament that will work for a less experienced rider. That is not the norm however. In getting a younger horse, consider having the help of an experienced trainer.

A 12 to 15 year-old horse may be safer. It should have a lot of riding years on those hooves and will be a more savvy trail horse, or at least should have a good deal of training. This horse should be your partner for a good 10 years or more.

As a rule, mares are more challenging than geldings. (Only an experienced horse handler should consider buying a stallion.) Mares "come in season" about once a month for most of the year. For many, the hormonal changes of estrus cause behavioral changes that can make them more difficult to handle and train during those periods. Mares do not go through menopause so dealing with their hormones doesn't end with a certain age. (There are medications that can help in more severe cases.) Generally speaking, mares show more personality and affection. Younger geldings tend to play and nip.

So age and sex will point you towards your new horse. Next, you will be looking for a breed of horse that will be best for the type of riding activities you like best. Having some knowledge and experience with different breeds is very helpful. When you start going to look at available horses, take a knowledgeable horse owner with you if possible.

One caveat about choosing a horse: Pretty is as pretty does. If you fall in love with a gorgeous horse but it has no training or a nasty temperament, pretty isn't worth a dime. Sometimes the more homely animals are dreams to handle and ride.

Places to look for a horse include the free publication, "The Horse Trader," which can be found in many tack stores and also online. Also, at local stables ask the manager or the trainers if they know of any horses for sale. There are horses listed at various sites online, including by breed or as rescue animals.

It will be helpful to have some knowledge of good horse confirmation so that you recognize obvious problems. For example the fetlocks should sit at a particular angle. If they are deeply dropped, it can indicate a serious problem that will make the horse unrideable. Confirmation can even affect how a horse "travels" so that a particular horse may be perfectly sound but not built for the job you want it to do.

When you go to look at a horse, have the owner handle and ride it first. Pay attention to what you see. Then ask if you can be allowed to handle the horse. Ask the seller to take off the saddle and then proceed with your examination and evaluation of the animal:

- Look at the head and eyes. Are the eyes clear? Any sign of irritation? Horses can have chronic conditions that cause their eyes to run tears.

- Look at the hooves, front and back. Do they seem well formed, solid not dry or cracked. Are there any blemishes that would indicate an injury?

- Run you hands down all four of the horse's legs. Of course check with the seller to be sure the horse isn't sensitive and that this is safe. Look for swelling and also for bony lumps where there shouldn't be any. (Those knots on the inside of the knees are called "chestnuts" and are normal. They grow and then drop off on a continuous basis.)

- Ask for a grooming brush and run it over the horse's body. Is it sensitive when you do this? The coat should be shiny and soft, not dull and brittle.

- Now ask for a tail brush and groom the horse's tail, assuming it is safe to do so. Note that some horses just don't like to be groomed. It is ticklish or just annoying and they squirm, try to nip you, whip their tail around, etc. It won't be fun working with a horse like that over the years.

- Pick the horse's feet. It should willingly lift its hooves and hold them up with support until you are finished.

- Now lead the horse around a bit. A horse with good ground manners is paying attention to you. It respects your space. It doesn't crowd you. It stops when you stop and it takes a cue from your body language when you want to turn so that very little pressure is needed on the halter. This will be your first clue about the animal's temperament and training.

- Now ask to saddle the horse yourself. Is it "cinchy?" A cinchy horse is annoyed with what you are doing and will reach its head around in a threatening manner.

- Bridle the horse yourself. It should willingly accept the bit and allow you to slip the bridle over it's head.

- When you ride the horse, check that it "has brakes!" That is, that it stops easily on command. You may have to learn the horse's other cues. But stopping shouldn't be something you have to second guess.

There may not be time in some situations to figure that out.

Before you make an offer on any horse, be sure you are totally comfortable handling and riding it. If you are not, keep looking.

Something to beware of is a horse that might be "too good to be true." For instance, a younger horse of one of the hotter breeds such as an Arabian or Andalusian or Thoroughbred that is ultra calm. It is not uncommon for a seller to dope the horse with something that calms it down. These products can even be bought over the counter. Under these circumstances you are not seeing the real horse, the one you will find when you get it home. This can happen at horse auctions or if a seller is in a hurry to sell the animal.

When you find a horse that you really are interested in, consider an offer to lease the horse for the first month so that you can make sure it is the right one for you. You may be able to leave the horse where it is and pay a lease fee. Then, for that month spend as much time as possible handling and riding the horse. Often owners will agree to this arrangement because they want the best outcome for the animal and want to make sure the placement is good for both the horse and the buyer. After a month, you will have a fair picture of what you are about to purchase. If you feel you are the luckiest person in the world, it's the right decision. If you feel unsure about it, keep looking.

An important aspect to keep in mind as you look for your perfect horse: Don't expect you can make a bad horse good if you just put in enough time. By bad, I mean a horse that spooks, a horse that bucks, a horse that bites or intimidates you. Some behaviors might be improved or corrected, but do you really need to take the chance that these behaviors won't change?

(Physically, horses do improve and change. So a rescue horse that is thin with a coarse coat can become beautiful or handsome after it gains weight and is fed a proper diet. Generally speaking, horses have an amazing capacity to heal many wounds, injuries, and weight loss given time. Once they feel better, they might become quite spunky too.)

Once you are sure you have found the horse for you, consider having a "vet check" before you make an offer on the horse. Sometimes, the seller will agree to pay for the vet check if the horse fails it. Or, you can ask the seller to at least split the cost of a basic check up. If you want the legs x-rayed, that's a cost you'll need to pay. If the horse is older and not expensive, you may decide to skip the vet check and expect to cover the cost of whatever problems arise over time. If you skip a vet check, the seller may agree to release the vet records. This will show you the medical issues and general health of the animal.

With an older horse, say seventeen years and up, the horse may have issues with arthritis, ring bone, teeth problems, Cushings disease, etc. Treating these will add up over time but hopefully won't break the bank and you can still have a good trail horse for many years. If you are buying a younger horse and plan to compete with it, the cost of a vet check will help guarantee you are getting a horse healthy enough for that.

These are just some of the things that are important when picking a horse. Have a trainer or someone experienced accompany you as you look at horses. Listen to their advice. Don't let the romance of having a horse outweigh the reality of having to deal with the wrong horse.

* * * * * * * * * * * * * * *

My Story:

A friend was ready to buy her first horse. She was a "senior citizen" who had never owned one. First, she took lessons and then she leased a horse. After six months of leasing, she knew she wanted her own horse.

She asked me to accompany her as she started her search. We went to a local ranch that was in the business of selling horses. My friend had called the owner first to advise we would be coming and what she was looking for.

When we got there the owner told my friend she had a 15-year-old mare and a 19-year-old gelding that were probably suitable, the right price and dependable. My friend had already decided she wanted a gelding. She had seen and heard about the challenges a mare might present.

The offered gelding was tied to the rail when we arrived. He sure wasn't anything to look at. He was thin with a coarse coat. On the ranch, he was subjected to the weather in a large open pasture. Also, he had issues with his teeth and was not able to chew the hay. The ranch owner explained that she had owned the horse for 10 years and he was leased out every summer, mostly to children's summer camps that offered riding.

The first thing I did was untie the horse to lead him around. He was not interested in being petted, and turned his head away slightly. He wasn't about to make any immediate attachments given his camp history of so many riders over the years.

What I found was a horse with amazing ground manners. The absolute best I had ever experienced in 20 years of handling horses. I pointed this out to my friend and told her this could well be the horse for her. A horse that is so responsive to you while you are working with it on the ground is very likely to be excellent under saddle. And that was what we found. She did buy the horse and he was absolutely perfect for her, a beginner horse owner who is cautious and needed a very dependable animal.

When my friend got her horse home, she changed him to a pelleted feed, kept him sheltered, made sure he had the best she could give him. A year later he looked and acted like a new horse. He was the perfect weight, his coat was shiny, and he nickered to us every time we arrived at the stables. A success story for both the owner and the horse.

NOTES

VII.

BRINGING YOUR HORSE HOME

This is an exciting moment. You are bringing a wonderful animal home and into your life. It is the culmination of a process you started many months, even years, ago.

At this point, I can't emphasize the issue of safety enough. Your safety must be uppermost in your mind, always. Many sports activities involve risk, such as skydiving, scuba diving, skiing, rock climbing, and so forth. Handling and riding a horse is inherently risky. You can never eliminate your risk, but you can reduce it. Truthfully, many horse owners have experienced one injury or another, but there are those who have never broken a bone or had a serious injury. Your use of good judgment and a thoughtful approach to handling your horse may make the difference. So don't rush into anything as you go about enjoying your horse.

Here are some important safety points that I hope you will incorporate into your daily routine so that it becomes "second nature" when you are spending time with your horse, starting from day one.

1. Until you know your horse well, don't hang out in its stall. If you are in the stall with your horse, be aware of what is going on around you and have the horse face you. Make sure there is room so that the horse has a choice to avoid you if it is startled.

2. Each day as you arrive at your horse's stall, immediately assess your horse's health and demeanor. Proceed accordingly. (If you have a concern about the animal's health, ask a trainer or call your vet.)

3. As you get your horse out, and always while you handle it, teach and insist on good ground manners. Do not allow your horse to invade your space or pull you forward. It must go the pace that you ask and stop when you stop. It should not threaten other horses.

4. Tie your horse to the rail or tie up spot, leaving plenty of space between it and any other horses. Start your grooming and continue to assess your horse's demeanor. Like people, horses can have days when they are not in a very good mood. You may want to just allow the horse to run freely in the round pen or walk for a while on the hot walker before deciding to ride it.

5. Until you know your horse well, plan to start every ride by doing ground work on a lunge line first. Reinforce that the horse must walk, trot, canter and stop on your command. Read about desensitizing exercises and practice them. Do not discontinue your ground work until you are satisfied that your horse is showing you obedience and respect. If you are not very sure and comfortable that this is the case, tie the horse to the rail for a while and then take it back into the round pen. Do not ride until the horse is behaving.

6. When you saddle up, check all of your equipment to ensure it is in good condition and working order. Do

not take for granted that the equipment that worked yesterday will work today. Leather deteriorates and can rip apart. Screws in the bridle can come loose, and reins can come loose.

7. Always wear a helmet when riding, regardless of the style or type of equine activity you are planning. Some people are extra cautious and put the helmet on before taking the horse out of the stall.

8. Until you become a skillful rider and know your horse well, do not ride alone. Whether trail riding or in an arena, always ride with other horses and riders. This will contribute to your horse's feeling of the security of the herd. Also, if there should be any mishap there will be others there to assist you.

9. Do not take unwise or unnecessary risks, such as galloping with a group on the trail. Horses become excited in this circumstance, they may bolt or buck.

10. If you plan to trailer out to unfamiliar trails, scout them out first. And, while riding, if you come to an area on the trail that is too challenging, turn back. If a situation makes you uncomfortable, or your horse uncomfortable, don't do it.

11. Don't let your horse crowd other horses. Some horses are okay with another horse close behind, but many object and will kick. That kick could hit your horse or even hit you, and a painful injury may be the result. If your horse kicks routinely, tie a red ribbon on its tail as a warning to others.

12. Think twice (even three times) before deciding to ride when it is windy or stormy. Wind whips trees around, blows debris across the ground and up into the air and can easily spook your horse. All the sounds and motion will likely put your horse on alert and start its adrenaline flowing. This is a recipe for injury.

13. Be mindful of ropes and halters. Keep them away from your horse's feet as you tie up, bridle, etc. Tie the horse short enough that it will not step on the rope accidentally and long enough that it will not feel like its head is restricted. Don't let halters fall on the ground where your horse can step in it and get tangled up. These situations can cause a horse to panic and result in injury.

For the first few days, after bringing your horse to its new home, keep a close watch on it. Some horses will settle promptly and be fine. Others may not. Your horse may seem restless and call to other horses. This behavior should disappear in a few days. Be sure to monitor that the horse is eating and drinking. Rarely, but occasionally, a horse stops eating and drinking and may have to be returned to its prior owner. Worse however, a horse that is so anxious and not drinking can colic and become very ill.

It is a good idea to wait a day or two before riding your horse in its new surroundings. Use those days to walk the horse on a lead line and show it around the stables.

Using a hot walker can be a useful activity for your horse. If your stables has one, try your horse on it to determine that it knows how to behave and accepts the continuous walking, without stopping. Generally speaking, fifteen minutes in each direction should be sufficient and can be used as exercise, warm up, or cool down.

Continue taking lessons with a trainer if at all possible and follow your coach's advice. ALWAYS consult your trainer before you try a new activity with your horse. For example you may see others doing pole bending or barrel racing and think it looks like fun. That activity may not be suitable for your level of skill or your horse's temperament. Doing something new and athletic can excite your horse and result in unsafe behavior for you. (You may ask your trainer to ride the horse first in the new activity to judge how it will behave, and to give you lessons on how to ride that activity.)

Some new owners want to share their horse with friends and family or local children. The owners are very happy to have made a dream come true, and now they want to let others have a taste of the dream. They put those others ahead of the best interests of the horse, and truthfully ahead of their own best interests. Unless your horse was a "lesson horse" it won't be used to having multiple other riders. When you bring your horse home, it is important to let your horse bond with you. It will be learning about you and how you give it cues and what you expect. To put others on your horse can be confusing. Wait until you have had the horse long enough for it to see you as its leader, and for you to be confident that you know what to expect from your horse. Some trainers recommend that a horse have only one rider.

Some important reminders:

- A horse has a large bony head and a strong neck. If your horse swings its head around and knocks you in the jaw, you may need some serious dental care. So, just be aware of the horse's head. If working near it, put your hand on the cheek or neck so you know where it's head is.

- Horses are very sensitive and intuitive about their owner. If you are afraid of your horse it will pick up on this emotion. Fear is not the same as caution. Caution equals respect, and a horse understands that. Fear communicates that something is dangerous and a horse can become very anxious about it.

- Watch where you stand so you don't get stepped on. Horses don't do that intentionally, but it happens if the handler is careless. A thousand pounds on your foot hurts!

- Proceed deliberately and build confidence! A horse is much more comfortable and respectful if the owner is confident in what they are doing. Confidence is communicated to your horse when you know what you are doing, and when you let the horse know it must behave. Practice with handling horses is the only way to build confidence. Ask for supervision until you build that confidence.

- Learn and practice
    - haltering
    - enforcing good ground manners
    - lunging in the round pen or arena

- all aspects of good grooming
- saddling and cinching
- bridling
- riding skills necessary to employ that reduce the chance of an accident

* * * * * * * * * * * * * * *

My Story:

As an adult, when I got back into having a horse I read as much as possible. I subscribed to many different magazines about the horse world. I bought some books on the subjects that interested me. Now, you can also find so much online with your computer. Many people purchase videos that demonstrate various skills. Watching a trainer is a good way to learn. I was able to go to seminars and clinics in addition to watching the videos.

With Shadow, I was with a group of riders that were more experienced and I learned by watching, doing, and asking a lot of questions. With Doll, as soon as I purchased her I started working with a trainer. I worked with several trainers over the years while we were showing. They taught me invaluable lessons, some that really kept me out of trouble too!

NOTES

VIII.

IT'S TIME TO HAVE SOME FUN!

Much of this book has been instructive and focused on safety. The purpose for this is to inform the first-time horse owner so that the worst-case scenarios involving injury can be avoided. Now it's time to talk about some of the wonderful activities you can enjoy with a horse!

Over the 20 years of my horse ownership, I have had so much fun. If you can connect with a group of people who are adventurous and knowledgeable, you will do things with your horse that maybe you never even dreamt of. That was my good fortune.

As I mentioned, with Doll I did Western Pleasure horse shows. These take a lot of work, but it is so rewarding to be handed a blue ribbon. The day before the show you will be bathing your horse, clipping whiskers and ear hairs, polishing your saddle and so forth. You will want a good- looking outfit to wear too! I love my western hats. At the show you will sign up for the classes you want to show in. If a class involves a pattern, you will need to study it so you can perform it when it is your turn. Doll especially liked the classes with patterns and the trail obstacle courses. The point is precision riding and it is very challenging.

With Doll, working cows was a hoot! One of the skills is called "sorting." The cows (usually young ones), have numbers pasted on their backs and the horse and rider teams have to work through the numbers in order, 0 through 9. It is not easy to find the numbered cow, separate it from the herd and chase it away down the arena. Doll was never afraid of the cows and would reach down to nip their backsides as she chased after them. She was a herder just like a sheep dog!

Another fun activity is camping with your horse. There are sites that have been developed for this and there are corrals and watering barrels provided. You will bring your horse's feed and your equipment. Usually there are campfire arrangements and picnic tables. If you are lucky, there will be public showers and restrooms! From the campsite you will have trails to go on and usually beautiful scenery to enjoy.

With my horse, Shadow, I did parades, "trail trials," and even a Renaissance faire. At the faire, a group of us were the queen's entertainment. On horseback, we competed in games with the queen's entourage as our audience. We were dressed in costumes of the period with the women wearing flowing dresses.

Shadow was so good in parades. The Christmas parades are especially fun. The crowds are in such good cheer and the children love the horses. You do need a horse that won't be afraid of all the hoopla, bands playing and floats, etc.

Trail trials are a competition that takes place on actual riding trails. Obstacles that must be faced by the horse and rider are set up by the group running the trial. Along the trail, at each obstacle there is a judge evaluating and scoring how you and your horse perform. For example, you may have to reach down and pick up a saddle bag, then trot a hundred feet and put it down. Or, you may have to back your horse down an incline. Scary things may jump out at you from behind a bush or tree. You may have to dismount, "ground tie" your horse (drop the reins and the horse stands still), then walk away.

One of the most unusual obstacles that Shadow and I had to face was a swim across a river. All of the competitors were surprised by this! Few had ever done it before. Shadow had to think about stepping into the water, but once she decided it was okay, we waded in and she started swimming. I just stayed in the saddle and rode with her across the river. I'll never forget how thrilling that was.

As a side story, Doll was good about crossing water but one time we were with a group that wanted to ride up the creek (not across it). The water got deeper. It started out ankle deep for the horses, then knee deep, and then I felt Doll floating! Her feet weren't touching the bottom. Well, she didn't like that at all. So, she decided to dive under! It was like riding a dolphin. I came out of the saddle and curled up on the bottom of the creek as she swam by. She scrambled up the bank, turned around and looked me as if to ask, "What just happened?" She was a good girl not to bolt home. We were both soaked but soon dried out. And, no, water won't hurt your saddle at all. It dries too and you won't see any difference.

Some stables hold "play days" for their boarders. At a play day the riders compete in barrel racing, pole bending and other games. The stables may also have a drill team that performs at rodeos or other events. The drill is a series of planned maneuvers done to music, usually at a canter but sometimes at a trot.

Doll and I are retired now. We mostly take leisurely trail rides and belong to a ladies trotting drill team. I hope you are getting the idea that having a horse can be a great activity for years and years. It involves a lifetime of learning, and also a lifetime of pleasure. It can be as simple or as challenging as you want.

I am wishing you all the best in your quest for the ideal horse and experience. Thank you so much for reading this book and taking it to heart. Here's to many happy days with your dream come true, your own horse.

IX.

QUIZ – SAFETY ALWAYS

Take this quiz to reinforce what you have learned. Answers are given below.

1) When I buy a horse,
   a) I just need to find one I can afford.
   b) It is most important that I think it is pretty.
   c) I need to take time for important preparations.
   d) It will be easy to know the right one.

2) There are many different kinds of horse-related activities, and
   a) I will be happiest if I find out what I enjoy most.
   b) I will be happiest doing what my friends do.
   c) Any horse can do what I want to do.
   d) None of the above.

3) I plan to ride on local trails and
   a) I don't need to take any riding lessons.
   b) My friends can show me the way.
   c) I will ride alone to be safest.
   d) I know on any trail there can be unexpected challenges that we will have to be prepared to deal with.

4) Until I am confident and experienced,
   a) I should always handle and ride my horse under supervision.
   b) I will have a friend handle and ride my horse.
   c) I will not worry about lessons.
   d) I can always ask someone if I have a question.

5) Leasing a horse
   a) is a good way to learn the demands a horse will make on my time and energy.
   b) will cost less than buying one.
   c) will help me find out about that breed.
   d) all of the above.

6) At a minimum, a horse requires
   a) shelter, feed, hoof care, vaccinations and parasite control, good training and exercise.
   b) a clean coat and shoes.
   c) someone that loves it.
   d) a pasture with other horses.

7) Regarding equine equipment
   a) I plan to find the cheapest I can because this is the least important factor in owning a horse.
   b) it is important that the equipment fits the horse and that I routinely check for loose or broken parts.
   c) it will come with the horse I buy.
   d) all of the above.

8) Saddle blankets and cinches
   a) must color coordinate with the horse.
   b) can cause sores on the horse if not properly fitted.
   c) only come in one size and one color.
   d) don't contribute to safety in any way.

9) In addition to the level of my experience and skill, when I buy a horse
   a) I will need to consider its age and training.
   b) I will need to consider its breed and gender.
   c) I will need to consider the job it will be doing.
   d) All of the above.

10) Grooming
   a) can be done once a week since horses clean themselves like a cat.
   b) doesn't help me develop any skill with my horse.
   c) only needs to be done if the horse looks dirty.
   d) should be done daily to keep the horse clean, to see if there are any sores that need attention, and to help me build confidence handling my horse.

11) Ground work
   a) is done only in a large arena.
   b) is done occasionally to fine tune the horse.
   c) can be done any time I am handling my horse and in a round pen to re-enforce our relationship.
   d) is only done with young horses.

12) A vet check
   a) is recommended before buying a horse.
   b) should be done monthly.
   c) is what I hand the vet after any service.
   d) Is probably a waste of time and money.

13) Troublesome equine behaviors
  a) only occur in stallions.
  b) Include biting, bucking, spooking, and intimidation.
  c) are easily corrected.
  d) don't happen once a horse is trained.

14) When I bring my horse home
  a) I will hang out in its stall until it gets to know me.
  b) I will leave it alone for the first week.
  c) I will share my horse with anyone who wants to ride it.
  d) I will assess its demeanor and health daily.

15) I can improve my safety
  a) by always wearing a helmet.
  b) by continuing to take lessons with a trainer.
  c) by avoiding unnecessary risks on rides and choosing not to ride on windy, stormy days.
  d) all of the above.

QUIZ ANSWERS

1. ***Answer C*** - For your safety and best horse experience, there is much to learn and do before buying your first horse.

2. ***Answer A*** - Take the time to find out what equestrian activity you enjoy the most, then find the right horse for what you want to do.

3. ***Answer D*** - Trail riding seems like the easiest activity; however, because unexpected things can occur, the rider needs to know how to ride well and how to handle a frightened horse.

4. ***Answer A*** - With a good instructor, you can learn quicker and become more confident.

5. ***Answer D*** - Leasing before buying is recommended for the first-time horse owner. You can learn a lot before making your investment in a horse.

6. ***Answer A*** - Feed, hoof care, vaccinations, parasite control training and exercise are proof that a horse is well loved.

7. ***Answer B*** - Proper, well-maintained equipment will insure that you and your horse are safe and comfortable

8. ***Answer B*** - Blankets and cinches must fit or will cause sores that must heal before you can ride again.

9. ***Answer D*** - Depending on your experience and plans, when you buy your first horse be sure to consider factors such as age, training, breed, and gender.

10. ***Answer D*** - Don't under estimate the value of grooming your horse. Besides cleanliness, you will build confidence handling your horse and can use that time to evaluate your horse's overall condition and mood.

11. ***Answer C*** - Anytime you are handling your horse it is an opportunity to reinforce ground manners.

12. ***Answer A*** - A vet check prior to purchasing a horse will help guarantee the animal is suitable for what you plan to do with it.

13. ***Answer B*** - Biting, bucking, spooking and intimidation are troublesome, dangerous behaviors, and you are wise to pass on a horse that exhibits or is known to have a history of these behaviors.

14. ***Answer D*** - Assess your horse daily to determine any health issues and before riding to determine if the horse's behavior is normal.

15. ***Answer D*** - You are responsible for your safety and when you are with horses should always wear a helmet, always check out unfamiliar trails either on foot personally or by asking about them, and avoid riding on windy or stormy days.

YEAR ONE HEALTH RECORD

Veterinarian Name and Phone: ________________________
Farrier Name and Phone: ____________________________

Vaccination Type: ____________________ Date: ____________
Vaccination Type: ____________________ Date: ____________
Vaccination Type: ____________________ Date: ____________
Vaccination Type: ____________________ Date: ____________
Vaccination Type: ____________________ Date: ____________

Teeth Exam/Floating Date: ________________

Worming Type: ______________________ Date: ____________
Worming Type: ______________________ Date: ____________
Worming Type: ______________________ Date: ____________
Worming Type: ______________________ Date: ____________

Hoof Care: _________________________ Date: ____________
Hoof Care: _________________________ Date: ____________
Hoof Care: _________________________ Date: ____________
Hoof Care: _________________________ Date: ____________
Hoof Care: _________________________ Date: ____________
Hoof Care: _________________________ Date: ____________
Hoof Care: _________________________ Date: ____________

Miscellaneous: ______________________ Date: ____________
Miscellaneous: ______________________ Date: ____________
Miscellaneous: ______________________ Date: ____________
Miscellaneous: ______________________ Date: ____________

Heart Rate (Normal = 28 to 44 beats per minute) ____________
Temperature (Normal = 99.5 to 101.5)__________________
Respiration (Normal = 10 to 18 breaths per minute) __________
Gums: Should be pale pink
Gut Sounds: Two to four small gurgles per minute
One large rumble every two to three minutes

Printed in Great Britain
by Amazon

81591927R00037